Celebrating Cranberries

.....a collection of cranberry

recipes

Fern Walker

Enjoy!

Fern Walker

Published by *Walkerworks*,
Ashton, Ontario
K0A 1B0
(613)257-5009
ISBN 0-9684596-0-9

Printed and bound in Canada

Foreword

Wearing red and talking about cranberries is something new for this "dyed-in-the-wool Blueberry girl"! But like the wild blueberries, cranberries are also a perfect source of anthocyanins (antioxidants that help fight the war against free radicals in our bodies, which can trigger cancer and heart disease.)

We have been blessed with many natural fruits and vegetables; one thing that we can do to help ourselves enjoy a better quality of life is to use these God-given treasures more often.

Cranberries are full of vitamins, calcium, iron, potassium, magnesium and many other trace minerals. They ARE good for us, so let's celebrate cranberries by incorporating them into our daily menus.

Enjoy !

Fern Walker

Thanks to everyone who assisted in the production of this book—in particular, Jane Jones for layout and production; Jim Walker for design and photography; Jill Walker for typing; and Gail Baird for her enthusiastic support and willingness to help at every turn in the road.

Thanks to Oxford Frozen Foods for supplying all the berries used in testing each recipe (sometimes more than once!) For doing a lot of testing in her kitchen, we thank Bette Maidment and her family who were great Food Judges! Also, a big thank you to all our friends who shared their favourite recipes for this book.

A special thank you to my family who took on extra tasks and turned a blind eye to the stacks of baking pans in the kitchen every night. They all have been a fantastic support system—thanks, Paul, Julia, Jill, Jim, Amy, Tom and Jane !

This book is dedicated to the memory of my Grandmother, Mabel Rose Stonehouse who patiently taught me to cook and always encouraged me to try new things with confidence; and to my Mother, Louise Hope Stonehouse, who gave a young teenager charge of weekly stocking the pantry to include the ingredients needed to bake special treats to entertain my friends. Thank you Mom!

CONTENTS

Metric Conversions

1/4 tsp.	1 mL
1/2 tsp.	2 mL
3/4 tsp.	4 mL
1 tsp.	5 mL
1 1/4 tsp.	6 mL
1 1/2 tsp.	7 mL
1 3/4 tsp.	8 mL
2 tsp.	10 mL
2 1/2 tsp.	12 mL
3 tsp.	15 mL
1 tbsp.	15 mL
2 tbsps.	30 mL
1/8 cup	25 mL
1/4 cup	50 mL
1/3 cup	75 mL
1/2 cup	125 mL
2/3 cup	150 mL
3/4 cup	175 mL
1 cup	250 mL
1 1/4 cup	300 mL
1 1/3 cup	325 mL
1 1/2 cup	375 mL
1 3/4 cup	425 mL
2 cups	500 mL
3 cups	750 mL

Starters

Jill's Christmas Punch

1 bottle   cranberry cocktail
1 large can   unsweetened pineapple juice
1 large can   frozen orange juice
2 bottles   carbonated drinks (usually ginger
                       ale or for a sweeter punch use 7up)

Cranberry-Cider Punch

8 cups   fresh apple cider
8 cups   cranberry ginger ale
1/2 cup   frozen whole cranberries
1   orange sliced
1   lemon sliced
1   lime sliced
1 can   frozen raspberry juice — unthawed
                  (optional)

Stir all together in punch bowl. Leave frozen raspberry unthawed so it will chill punch

1.

Christmas Wassail

1 bottle	cranberry cocktail (64 oz.)
1 can (12 oz.)	fozen pineapple juice
1 can (12 oz.)	frozen pink lemonade
3 cups	water

At this stage it can be served cold, as a punch. If heating, add 3 cinnamon sticks, and bring to a boil, then simmer (covered) for 1 hour.

Jingle Bell Punch

20   seedless green grapes
4 cups   white grape juice
4 cups   cranberry juice
4 cups   ginger ale

Place grapes on small plate — cover with saran and freeze for at least 2 hours (up to 2 days).

In a pitcher or bowl, stir together juices. Just before serving, add the carbonated drink and pop the frozen grapes into each glass before pouring.

Bette's Breakfast Cup

1 cup	cranberries
1	thinly sliced orange
1/2	thinly sliced lemon
1 tbsp.	lemon juice
1/2	stick cinnamon
1 cup	water

Simmer all of the fruit in half of the water for 20 minutes.

> **1 fresh pink grapefruit (sectioned and slice)**
> **1/2 cup sugar**
> **1/2 tsp. salt**

Add this to the first mixture and bring to a boil.

2 tsp. cornstarch — Mix with the other 1/2 cup of water and add to mixture till it thickens a bit. CHILL. Dribble plain yogourt on top prior to serving. If you dare, try serving this as a soup.!

4.

Jellied Salad

1 pkg   lime jello (lg.)
few drops green food colouring
1 cup   boiling water
2 tbsp.   vinegar
1 sm. can crushed pineapple (drained)
1/2 cup   grated cranberries

Stir jello into boiling water, mix well. Add 2 tbsp,
vinegar, and set aside to cool. Grate or grind the
cranberries and mix with the crushed pineapple.
When jello begins to firm up a bit, stir in fruit and
refrigerate. Unmould just before serving.

Carrot Salad

3 cups   shredded carrots
1   med. orange, peeled and sectioned
3 tbsp.   lemon juice
1/2 cup   chopped cranberries
2 tbsp.   sugar
dash   salt
1/2 cup   raisins
dash   cinnamon

Let sit in regfrigerator to marinate for at least 2 hours. If not wet enough, add a little cranberry vinegar and oil (2 tbsp of each).

Cranberry Vinegar on Page 10.

6.

Cranberry Salad Cups

1 cup	crushed pineapple
9	pineapple slices
1 pkg.	raspberry gelatin
1/4 cup	sugar
1 tbsp.	lemon juice
1 cup	ground cranberries
1tbsp	small orange ground (quartered & seeded)
1 cup	celery finely chopped
1/2 cup	walnuts (optional)

Drain both kinds of pineapple, save juice. Add water to juice to make 2 cups. In a saucepan, combine sugar, gelatin and water. Over low heat, stir till dissolved. Add lemon juice. Chill. When partially set, add ground fruits, crushed pineapple, celery and nuts. Pour into 8 or 9 custard cups or paper cups, (moulds). Chill till firm. Unmould onto the pineapple rings which have been placed on lettuce leaves. Top with dollops of mayonaise, May be decorated with a few tiny lettuce leaves.

Cranberry Sauce
(Traditional)

3 cups   cranberries
2 cups   sugar
1 cup   water

In a saucepan bring to boil, then reduce heat, and cook for 10 minutes. Cool, bottle, and refrigerate.

Baked Cranberry Sauce

2 cups   cranberries (washed & stemmed)
           or frozen I.Q.F.
1 1/2 cups sugar
1   orange, thinly sliced
3/4 cup   cup orange juice

Heat oven to 350° — bake 1 hour. Layer ingredients in a casserole dish and bake, uncovered. Sauce will thicken as it cools.

8.

Norma's Cranberry Relish

1 pkg.   cranberries (2 1/2 cups)
2   apples
2   oranges
2   lemons
2 cups   sugar (or to taste)

Take rough ends off and take seeds out, but don't peel fruit.
Process in food processor.
Taste for sugar.
Ready to serve. (freezes well).

9.

Cranberry Vinegar

2 1/2 cups cranberries
1 1/3 cups sugar
1 1/2 cups vinegar
1 1/2 cups water
2   sticks cinnamon

Bring to a boil, then simmer about 5-7 minutes (or till berries burst). Cool. Strain through a fine sieve into jars. At this point, split the vinegar, and add herbs of your choice and perhaps mint to the other half. Or, you can leave it all plain. When using in salads, just add a bit of sugar and equal amounts of oil and vinegar.

Muffins and Breads

Cranberry Corn Muffins

1/4 cup	unsalted butter (melted)
3/4 cup	flour
1/2 cup	cornmeal
1 1/2 tsp.	baking powder
1/2 cup	sugar
1 tbsp.	grated lemon peel
1/2 cup	milk
2	eggs, beaten
1/2 cup	cranberries

Mix together in order given.
Bake at 400° for 25 minutes.

Amy's Cranberry Relish Muffins

1 1/2 cups flour
1/4 cup white sugar
2 tsp. baking powder
1/2 tsp. salt
1/4 cup butter or margarine
1 cup plain yogourt
1/4 cup milk
1 egg
1/2 tsp. vanilla
1 cup Cranberry relish (make sure it is sweet enough. Add more sugar if necessary). (see pg. 9 for Cranberry Relish)

Blend dry ingredients. Melt butter (micro proof bowl) in microwave. Add yogourt and milk and blend. Beat in egg and vanilla. Add butter mixture to dry ingredients and stir until moistened. Add cranberry relish and stir. Spoon into a well-greased muffin tin. Bake at 375° for 15-20 minutes.

* the yogourt makes these moist and yummy!
12.

Streusel Muffins

3 cups	flour
2 tbsps.	baking powder
1/2 tsp.	salt
1 cup	sugar
1/2 cup	butter
2	eggs, beaten
1 cup	milk
1 cup	halved cranberries
1/2 cup	chopped pecans
2 tbsps.	sugar
1 tbsp.	grated lemon peel

Heat oven to 400°. Mix ingredients in order given. Cut butter into dry ingredients. Add milk and eggs together, just until batter is holding together. Stir in cranberries and pecans. Spoon into muffin tins, 2/3 full, Mix lemon peel and sugar together, and sprinkle on top of muffins. Bake at 400° for 20 to 25 minutes.

Julia's Muffins

2 cups	flour
1 3/4 cups	bran
1/4 cup	oats
1 cup	sugar
2 tsp.	salt
2 cups	milk
2 tsps.	soda
2	eggs
3/4 cup	safflower oil
1 cup	frozen cranberries or frozen wild blueberries

Stir all dry ingredients together. Dissolve soda in milk. Whisk eggs, oil and milk together. Stir into dry mixture. Add fruit gently and put into greased muffin tins to 3/4 full. Bake at 400° approx. 20 minutes or till browned.

* Tip — add fruit still frozen - batter is not so likely to become coloured with juice.

Jiffy Cranberry Muffins

1 1/2 cups	flour
1/2 cup	sugar
1 tsp.	baking soda
1 tsp.	baking powder
1/2 tsp.	salt
1 1/2 tsps.	cinnamon
2	eggs
3/4 cup	oil
1 cup	chopped cranberries

Heat oven to 400°. Mix all dry ingredients together.
Then add beaten eggs and oil. Fold in cranberries,
spoon into greased muffin tins and bake at 400° for
20 minutes.

Aunt Anne's Orange Bread

1 1/4 cups sugar
1/2 cup shortening, melted
2 eggs
1 1/2 tsps. baking powder
1/2 tsp. salt
2 cups flour
1/2 cup fresh orange juice
1 cup cranberries
  grated orange rind
2 tbsps. warm water

Heat oven to 350°. Combine sugar with all dry ingredients. Beat eggs, add juice, shortening and water.
Add dry ingredients, then cranberries and orange
rind. Spoon into greased, lined loaf pans. Bake
approx. 1 hour. Cool 10 minutes, then turn out on
wire rack. Remove waxed paper, then continue to
cool.

16.

Pumpkin-Cran Bread

2 cups	sugar
1 cup	oil
4	eggs
2 cups	pumpkin
1 cup	cranberries, chopped
3 cups	flour
2 tsps.	baking powder
2 (scant) tsps.	soda
1/4 tsp.	salt
2 tsps.	cinnamon

Heat oven to 350°. Blend together oil, sugar and eggs. Stir in pumpkin. Mix the dry ingredients and stir into first mixture. Add cranberries last. If desired — 1/2 cup raisins and/or nuts may be added here. Spoon into greased rectangular pan and bake at 350° approx. 1 hour.

Mom's Cranberry Nut Bread

2 cups	flour
1 cup	sugar
1 1/2 tsps.	baking powder
1/2 tsp.	soda
1 tsp.	salt
1/4 cup	shortening
3/4 cup	orange juice
1 tbsp.	grated orange rind
2	eggs, well beaten
2 cups	cranberries (chopped)
1/2 cup	nuts (chopped)

Sift together the dry ingredients, then cut in shortening until mixture resembles coarse cornmeal. Combine orange juice and grated rind with the well-beaten egg. Pour all at once into dry ingredients mixing just 'til moist. Carefully fold in nuts and cranberries. Spoon batter into a greased loaf pan and BAKE at 350° — about one hour (until crust is golden).
For Christmas, halve the cranberries, add 2/3 cup halved green cherries, and omit the nuts.

18.

Cran-Orange Bread

Peel from 2 oranges *
2 1/4 cups sifted flour
3/4 cup sugar
3 tsps. baking powder
1 tsp. salt
1 cup chopped cranberries
1 cup milk
2 beaten eggs
3 tbsps. butter (melted)

First: Prepare orange peel — cut peel in thin strips then lay several strips together and chop finely.

Sift together flour, sugar, baking powder and salt. Add orange peel and cranberries. Combine eggs, milk and melted butter. Add all at once to the dry ingredients, stirring just until flour is moistened. Bake at 350° for one hour.

* Save oranges for a salad

Alma's Cranberry Loaf

2 cups	all purpose flour
1 cup	sugar
1 1/2 tsps.	baking powder
1 tsp.	salt
1/2 tsp.	baking soda
1/4 cup	butter/margarine
1 egg	beaten
1 tsp.	grated orange peel
3/4 cup	orange juice
1 to 1 1/2 cups	light raisins
1 1/2 cups	cranberries

Put dry ingredients (first five) in bowl. Then cut in butter until mixture is crumbly. Add egg, orange peel and juice all at one time. Stir until mixture is evenly moist (not too much). Fold in raisins and cranberries. Spoon into greased 9"x 5" x 3" loaf pan. Bake at 350° for 1 hour and 10 minutes.

Cranberry Scones

2 cups	flour
4 tsps.	baking powder
1/2 tsp.	salt
2 tbsps.	sugar
1/2 cup	margarine or shortening or butter
2/3 cup	milk
3/4 cup	chopped cranberries
1/4 cup	raisins (optional)
1/4 cup	sugar

Heat oven to 425 degrees. Combine dry ingredients. Cut in the margarine/shortening/butter. Dredge the cranberries and raisins with sugar. Stir fruit into batter, then add milk. Stir and knead about 10 times. Roll out dough on floured board, cut out scones and place on baking sheets. Bake at 425 degrees for 10-12 minutes. For nicely browned tops, dot the top of scones with a teaspoon of cream just before baking.

Gram's Christmas Wreath Ring

2 cups	flour
4 tsps.	baking powder
pinch	salt
2 tbsps.	sugar
1/4 cup	butter
1 cup	cold milk
1 (8 oz.)	pkg. cream cheese, softened
1/4 cup	sugar
1/2 tsp.	vanilla
1/2 cup	cranberries (chopped)
1/2 cup	raisins (if raisins are dry, moisten in a little orange juice)
1/4 cup	pecans (optional)

Combine first four dry ingredients. Cut in butter till dough is crumbly. Then add milk gradually only until soft dough forms. Beat cheese, sugar and vanilla together. Roll out dough on floured board in a rectangular pattern. Spread cheese mixture over dough, then sprinkle fruit and nuts over cheese. Beginning at the long side, roll up and seal edges. Place on baking sheet and shape the "tube" of dough into a circle. Seal two ends. Snip along the roll with cuts half way through. Bake at 425° for 15 to 20 mins. (until crusty and golden). Brush with a little corn syrup if done for Christmas — add some green icing at the seam or maybe tie a red bow around it.

22.

Main Meals

Baked Chicken

6-8	breasts of chicken
2 tbsps.	margarine
1 cup	home made chili sauce
	(recipe on next page)
3/4 cup	home made cranberry sauce (page 8)

Preheat oven to 350°. In baking dish, melt margarine (2 mins). Arrange the chicken (bone side up) in the melted margarine. Cook for 20-25 minutes. Remove from oven, and turn chicken over. Cover with the chili sauce. Cook another 20-25 minutes. Stir cranberry sauce into the juices in the dish, and heat another 5 minutes. Serve, spooning sauce over each piece.

Jane's Chili Sauce

6	ripe tomatoes (peeled and chopped)
6	McIntosh apples (peeled, cored and chopped)
5	small onions (chopped)
2 tbsps.	salt
2 cups	sugar
1/2 tsp.	cinnamon
1/4 tsp.	cloves
1/4 tsp.	turmeric
1/4 tsp.	cayenne pepper
1 cup	vinegar

Bring to a boil and cook on simmer for approximately 45 minutes or so. When apples have mushed up and the colour is good, the chili is ready. Bottle in sterile jars and cover, when cooled, with parafin wax.

Chicken-Cranberry Layers

1st Layer: 1 tbsp. gelatin
1/4 cup cold water
2 cups cranberries
1 cup crushed pineapple
1/2 cup broken walnuts
1 tbsp. lemon juice

Soften gelatin in cold water. Dissolve over a pan of hot water. Add remaining ingredients. Pour into 10 x 6 x 1 1/2" baking dish. Chill till firm.

2nd Layer: 1 tbsp. gelatin
1/4 cup cold water
1 cup mayonaise
1/2 cup water
3 tbsps. lemon juice
3/4 tsp. salt
2 cups cubed cooked chicken
1/2 cup diced celery
2 tbsps. chopped parsley

Soften gelatin in cold water. Dissolve over a pan of hot water. Blend in next 4 ingredients. Add chicken, celery and parsley. Pour over cranberry layer. Chill. Cut in 6 to 8 squares and invert on lettuce. Top with a dollop of mayonaise and walnut halves.

Cranberry Stuffing

1/2 lb.	sausage meat
1/2 cup	chopped celery
1/2 cup	chopped onion
1/2 tsp.	savory
1/2 tsp.	sage
1/2 tsp.	salt
4 1/2 cups	bread crumbs
1-2 cans	chicken broth
1 cup	chopped cranberries

Sauté onions and celery. Brown the sausage meat in frying pan, and drain. Stir all together, add spices. Then tear up bread, or if using crumbs stir together. Mix in cranberries and pour over chicken broth. Press in baking pan, and cook at 350° for approx. 30 to 40 minutes. If you like it crusty, you can leave it in longer. Also, the difference between bread and crumbs may mean that you need to add more chicken broth.

This is good with pork as well as turkey.

Hope's Deluxe Salmon Casserole

1 large can	red salmon (save liquid)
1 cup	rice
2 tbsps.	butter
1/2 cup	chopped onion
2 tbsps.	chopped green pepper
1/2 cup	chopped cranberries
1 can (8 oz)	low-fat cream of mushroom soup
2/3 cup	salmon liquid mixed with milk
1 3/4 cups	potato chips
1/3 cup	blanched, thinly-sliced almonds

Cook rice. Drain and flake salmon (save liquid to mix with milk). Combine salmon with rice. Melt the butter and saute onion and green pepper till tender. Chop cranberries and stir in for a few minutes. Add to salmon mixture. Combine soup and liquid. Place half of the potato chips in a greased casserole and cover with alternate layers of salmon and soup mixture. Cover with remaining chips, sprinkle with almonds. Bake at 375° for 30 minutes or so.

Cranberry-Stuffed Salmon

1 cup	bread crumbs
1/4 cup	chopped celery (finely chopped)
1/4 cup	melted butter/margarine
1/4 cup	chopped cranberries
1/2 tsp.	sage
1/4 tsp.	savoury
1	small 3-4 lb Salmon (cleaned)

Wash cavity of salmon, and wipe dry. Tear up bread crumbs, chop celery and cranberries, sprinkle with sage and savoury, then toss with melted butter. Stuff into salmon and wrap it with waxed paper, covering thick end with double ply paper. Microwave on HIGH for 10 minutes (turning 1/2 way through.)

Peggy's Cranberried Meatballs

1 1/2 lbs.	lean ground beef
1	egg (beaten)
1/2 cup	fresh bread crumbs
dash	salt
dash	worcestershire sauce
1	small onion grated

Mix these ingredients all together and shape into small balls. Fry the balls until brown, then arrange in a large casserole dish. Bake at 350 degrees for about 15 minutes, then add following sauce:

> **1 cup chopped cranberries**
> **1/4 cup apple juice**
> **1/4 cup cider or red wine vinegar**
> **1/4 cup brown sugar**
> **2 tsp. Dijon mustard**

Cook these ingredients until thickened, then add to casserole dish and heat on low for 10 more minutes. (Makes about 45 meatballs).

Stuffed Pork Loin Roast

3-4 lbs.	boneless pork loin roast
1 tsp.	salt
1/4 tsp.	pepper
1/8 tsp.	garlic powder
1/4 tsp.	worcestershire sauce
1/2 cup	chopped cranberries
1/2 cup	chopped apricots
1/2 cup	chopped prunes
1/2 tsp.	cumin(optional)
1/2 tsp.	cinnamon
1 tsp.	grated orange rind

Heat oven to 325 degrees. Open roast out. Mix fruit with spices and rind, spoon it down centre of roast. Fold meat and tie with butcher's string. Combine salt, pepper, worcestershire sauce and rub outside of roast. If you wish a sweeter taste, you can rub it with brown sugar and mustard glaze instead . Bake in 325 oven for 45 minutes per pound.

Cranberried Sweet Potatoes

3 cups   sweet potatoes (cooked and mashed)
dash   salt
1/2 cup   butter
1/3 cup   milk

Spoon into a greased casserole dish.
Add:
1 cup   chopped cranberries OR 1 cup cranberry
            sauce (recipe on page 8).
2 tbsps.   brown sugar
1 tsp.   grated orange rind
2 tbsps.   melted margarine
1/2 cup   chopped pecans

Bake at 350° for 30-35 mins.

Alternate Sweet Potato

2 or 3   large sweet potatoes (cubed)
1 cup   cranberries (chopped)
Cover with: **1/2 cup** rolled oats
               1/2 cup flour
               1/2 cup brown sugar
               1 tsp. cinnamon

Bake at 350° for about 35 minutes.
Other Options: Pineapple slices give a different taste.

Acorn Squash (Microwave)

Cut the squash in halves. Bake (wrapped in Saran) at HIGH for 4 minutes.

Uncover and fill cavities with following mixture:

2 tbsps.	melted butter
2 tbsps.	brown sugar
pinch	of salt
dash	of nutmeg
1	diced, skinned pear
1/2 cup	chopped cranberries

Cover and cook again on HIGH for 4 minures

Desserts

Basic Pastry Recipe

6 cups   flour
1 lb   shortening
1   egg, beaten
1 tbsp.   vinegar
            iced water

Cut shortening into flour. Beat egg with a fork in a measuring cup, add vinegar to same cup and then fill to one cup with iced water. Roll out on floured board and knead gently just until dough holds together. Wrap balls of dough in waxed paper and refrigerate. This recipe makes enough pastry for 3 double crust pies.

Alternate Pastry Recipe
(For Tarts)

1 cup   butter (at room temperature)
6 oz.   cream cheese (at room temperature)
2 cups   regular flour

Beat butter and cream cheese until light and fluffy.
Add flour and stir with a wooden spoon until dough
forms a ball. Shape into 3 balls, wrap in waxed paper
and refrigerate.

When filling is ready, work with one ball at a time,
rolling out on a floured board. Cut into rounds and
press into mini muffin pans or tartlet pans.
Bake at 350°for 20 minutes. Good with the following fillings: mincemeat, butter tart filling, or the
cranberry pear (pg. 42)

Old-Fashioned Cranberry Pie

3 tbsps.	cornstarch
1/4 tsp	salt
1 1/2	cups sugar
1/4 tsp	nutmeg
2 1/2 cups	cranberries
1 cup	sliced apples
	(or 1 cup wild blueberries)
1 cup	water
1 1/2 tbsps.	butter (cut up)

Combine cornstarch, salt, sugar and nutmeg. Chop cranberries in half and add to dry ingredients, along with water. Pour into a pastry-lined pie plate, dot with pieces of butter and cover with a top crust, or a lattice top. Prick top with fork a few times and bake as follows: 450° oven for 15 minutes, then at 350° for last 35 minutes.

Jill R's Cranberry-Pecan Pie

3	eggs
1 cup	dark corn syrup
2/3 cup	sugar
dash	salt
4 tbsps.	melted butter
1 cup	chopped cranberries
1 cup	pecan halves
1	unbaked pie shell

Sprinkle cranberries and pecans over the unbaked pie shell. Mix the first five ingredients together, then pour over fruit. Bake at 325° for 55 minutes.

Gloria's Healthy Pie

6 tbsps. brown sugar
1/3 cup white sugar
1/3 cup flour
1/2 tsp. cinnamon
1/4 cup margarine
5 tbsps. milk
1 cup blueberries
1 cup raspberries
1 cup cranberries

Stir all dry ingredients together, then cut in margarine with a pastry blender. Add milk then toss fruit in 1 tablespoon of flour and place in unbaked pie shell. Dot top with a couple of pieces of butter and sprinkle 1 tablespoon of lemon juice over all. Cover with top pastry or a lattice top. Bake at 400°for 10 minutes then turn oven back to 350° and bake another 30 minutes or longer if needed.

No Crust Pie

2 tbsps.	butter
5 tbsps.	brown sugar
1tsp.	cinnamon
3	apples
1/2 cup	chopped cranberries
3/4 cup	flour
3	eggs
3/4 cup	milk
1/2 tsp.	salt

Melt butter in the bottom of a deep pie plate. Stir in the brown sugar and the cinnamon. Peel, core and slice apples. Layer them in the pie plate. Chop the cranberries in half and sprinkle over the apples. Bake in 425° oven for 10 minutes. Beat eggs with wooden spoon, add milk and salt. Stir in flour. Mix just till moist. Pour over the fruit in pie plate and bake for another 25 minutes. Dust with icing sugar or serve with ice cream.

Kay's Cran-Banana Delight

2 cups	cranberries
3	bananas (sliced)
1 cup	sugar
3-4 tsp.	cornstarch
	Unbaked pie shells.

Wash cranberries and put in a bowl. Slice bananas over top. Coat fruit with sugar & cornstarch. Fill pastry shell & cover with top crust or lattice top. Bake at 400° for 10 minutes, then reduce to 350° for 30 minutes.

Phyllo and Fruit Dessert

1/2 cup	butter
few tbsps.	sugar
7 sheets	phyllo pastry
Filling:	4 pears, peeled, cored, diced
1 cup	raisins
3 cups	frozen (IQF) cranberries
1 cup	sugar
1/2 cup	orange juice
1 tbsp.	water
1 tbsp.	cornstarch
1 tbsp.	grated orange rind

Combine prepared fruits, sugar and orange juice in cooking pot. Bring to a boil, then on Medium heat for 10 minutes. Mix cornstarch with water till dissolved and add to fruit-cook another minute or so. Stir in orange rind and let cool. Working with phyllo pastry: thaw package of dough- always keep the sheets covered while working (they dry out very quickly). Melt butter. Grease an 8" or 9" springform pan. Brush melted butter on first phyllo sheet and sprinkle with a little sugar. Put it over top of pan, letting edges hang over sides. Repeat this procedure with 3 more sheets, while rotating the pan 1/4 turn each time. Push all 4 layers gently down into centre of pan. Pour in cooled filling. Fold in pastry to cover. Layer remaining sheets of phyllo on top in same manner as before — buttering, sugaring and rotating pan. Fold the top sheet under the bottom and cut 3-4 vents on top. Bake at 400° for 30 minutes. If decorating, press 3 cut-up squares of phyllo into mini muffin tins while oven is still hot. Cook 6-7 minutes. Fill these with red currant jelly to attach (with dots of jelly) to top of dessert.

40.

Ulla's Linzer Torte

2 cups   flour
2/3 cups   sugar
1 tsp.   baking powder
1 tsp.   cinnamon
pinch   cloves
pinch   salt
1 cup   ground almonds
1 cup   butter
1   egg
2 1/2 cups prepared cranberries

Stir all dry ingredients together. Then cut in butter
and knead egg (beaten) into dough. Cool for 1 hour
in the refrigerator. Cook 1 1/2 cups of cranberries in
1 cup water and 1 cup sugar. Put 3/4 of dough in
greased spring form pan. Spread cranberries over
dough. Roll out remaining dough, cut strips and
make a lattice top. Bake at 350° for approximately
30 minutes.

Cranberry-Pear Crunch

4	*pears, peeled, cored and thinly sliced
1 cup	chopped cranberries
1/2 cup	raisins
1/2 cup	flour (divided)
1/2 cup	sugar
3/4 tsp.	cinnamon
1/4 tsp.	cloves
5 tbsps.	orange juice
6 tbsps.	butter or margarine (divided)
1/2 tbsp.	orange rind (grated)
2 cups	granola
3 tbsps.	brown sugar

Combine half of the flour with sugar, spices and fruit. Stir in orange juice, rind and 1 tablespoon of the softened butter. Spoon into buttered baking dish. Heat oven to 375°. Combine brown sugar, remaining flour and butter, cut in with pastry blender until crumbly. Add cereal, then sprinkle over fruit. Bake 30 minutes, then cover with foil for another 15 minutes. Great served with a scoop of vanilla ice cream.

* raspberries, apples and wild blueberries are a great substitute for the pears.

Alide's Whipped Delight (Roosamanna)

4 cups	cranberries
2 cups	water
2 tbsps.	lemon rind (grated)
2/3 cup	cream of wheat
1/2 cup	sugar
1/2 tsp.	vanilla

Cook cranberries in water approximately 10 minutes. Press through sieve. Add sugar to the juice, and the lemon peel, then bring to a boil. Sprinkle in the cream of wheat, mix briskly and simmer for 25 minutes, stirring occasionally. Pour into a large bowl and whisk till light (or electric beaters). Add vanilla. Chill for a half hour before serving.

Alide's daughter, Ruth, shared this family favourite with us as a loving tribute to her mother whom she says "used to make this by sight and taste".

Rhoda's Cranberry Cake

2 cups	flour
1 cup	sugar
1 tsp.	baking powder
1 tsp.	salt
	grated rind of 2 oranges
1 cup	buttermilk
2	eggs (beaten)
3/4 cup	safflower oil (or your own preference)
1 cup	whole cranberries
1 cup	dates
1 cup	chopped nuts (optional)
1/4 cup	flour

Combine the first eight ingredients well. Dredge the fruit in the quarter cup flour and stir into batter. Bake in a greased tube pan at 350° for one hour.

GLAZE: 1/4 cup butter
            1 cup icing sugar
            1 cup orange juice

Soften butter, and mix icing sugar into it. Stir orange juice into glaze. For a stiffer glaze, add more icing sugar as desired. Pour over cake a little at a time.

Nana's White Cake

3 cups   flour
2 cups   sugar
1 1/2 tsps. baking powder
1/2 tsp.   baking soda
1   lemon rind grated
1 cup   milk
3/4 cup   butter or margarine (melted)
3   eggs
1 cup   cranberries

Heat oven to 350°. Grease and flour bundt pan. Mix dry ingredients in large bowl. Add milk, butter and eggs. Beat on medium speed for 2 minutes. Stir in cranberries and spoon into prepared pan. Bake at 350° approximately one hour. Cool a few minutes then tilt bundt pan upside down, sticking a small kitchen funnel in the hole of the pan. When removed from pan, sprinkle with icing, or an almond glaze.

Glaze:
1 tbsp. butter
1 tsp. almond flavouring
1 1/2 cups icing sugar
1 tbsp. milk

Fruit Cake Alternative

4 cups	flour (keep 1/4 cup to dredge fruit)
2 cups	sugar
1 tsp.	baking powder
1 tsp.	baking soda
1/4 tsp.	salt
2	eggs, beaten
1 cup	orange juice
1/4 cup	shortening, melted
1/4 cup	water
1 1/2 cups	frozen cranberries, cut in halves
1 cup	chopped green cherries
2 slices	chopped candied pineapple
1 cup	golden raisins
1 cup	chopped dates
1 tbsp.	grated orange rind
1 1/2 cups	pecan halves

Measure dry ingredients together. Beat eggs and add melted shortening,water and juice. Stir in the dry ingredients until just combined. Fold in dredged fruit. Spoon into tube pan, or 2 (1 gram) loaf pans lined with waxed paper. Bake at 350 degrees for 1 hour or until toothpick comes out clean. Cool a few minutes, then turn out loaf pans and remove waxed paper carefully. If using a tube pan invert it, resting on a funnel and allow to cool.

46.

Different Butter Tart Squares

1/2 cup	butter
1 cup	sifted flour
2 tbsps.	sugar
1 1/2 cups	brown sugar
3 large	eggs (beaten)
3 tbsps.	flour
1/2 tsp.	baking powder
1 tsp.	vanilla
1 cup	chopped cranberries
1/2 cup	chopped pecans

Heat oven to 350°. Cream butter into flour and sugar. Press into 9" square pan (ungreased) and bake at 350 degrees for 15 minutes. Then mix all the other ingredients together, folding in cranberries and pecans last after filling is made. Spread evenly over base, return to oven and bake at 350° for another 20 minutes.

Gram's White Christmas Cookies

2/3 cup	butter or margarine
1 1/3 cups	brown sugar
2	eggs
3 cups	flour
2 tsps.	baking powder
1/4 tsp.	salt
1 tsp.	vanilla
1 cup	(approx) Basic Cranberry Sauce (Pg. 8)

Mix all ingredients together until well blended. Roll out dough on a floured board. Cut with round cookie cutters. Cut a doughnut hole in half of the cookies. Bake at 375° for 10 minutes. Remove from cookie sheets. Spread *Basic Cranberry Sauce* on the cookies without holes, cover them with the other cookies with holes. Press down. Sprinkle with icing sugar.

Sour Cream Cookies

1 cup	brown sugar
1/2 cup	shortening
1	egg, beaten
1/2 cup	sour cream
1/2 tsp.	salt
2 cups	pastry flour
1/2 tsp.	nutmeg
1/2 tsp.	soda
2 tsps.	baking powder
1 cup	chopped cranberries

Cream shortening and sugar together, add beaten egg
and cranberries. Stir dry ingredients together and
add to first mixture alternately with the sour cream.
Mix well, and drop by teaspoonfuls on greased
baking sheets. Bake in hot oven 400° for 15 minutes.

Special Cookies

1 cup	sugar
3/4 cup	brown sugar
1/2 cup	margarine or butter, softened
1/4 cup	milk
2 tbsps.	orange juice
1	egg
3 cups	flour
1 tsp	baking powder
1/2 tsp	salt
1/4 tsp	baking soda
1 1/2 cups	chopped cranberries
1 cup	white chocolate chunks
1/2 cup	chopped nuts (optional)

Heat oven to 375°. Mix sugars and butter in large bowl. Blend egg, milk and juice together, then add to sugar and butter. Stir dry ingredients together and then add to mixture. Drop spoonfuls of dough on greased cookie sheets and bake at 375° for approximately 12 minutes. Remove from cookie sheets and cool on wire racks.

Cran-Apple Sauce

1 1/2 cups   frozen cranberries
1 to 1 1/2 cups sugar
1 tsp   grated orange peel
3 cups   unsweetened applesauce
                    whipped cream - if desired

Bring cranberries and water (enough to cover) to a boil. Reduce heat and simmer until berries POP. Stir in sugar until dissolved and add orange peel. Refrigerate for 2 hours. Coarsley chop in a blender, stir in applesauce.

Cranberry Conserve

3 cups   cranberries
3   oranges (washed and seeded)
3   apples (washed and cored)
1 1/2 to 2 cups sugar per cup of fruit

Grind cranberries, oranges and apples. Add sugar and mix well. Store in jars in refrigerator.

Heather's Orange Cranberry Sorbet

1 1/2 cups cranberries (finely chopped)
2 cups water
3/4 cup sugar
1 envelope gelatin
3/4 cup orange juice
2 tbsps. Cointreau or Grand Marnier

Cook the cranberries in water for 10 minutes or so, until they are softened. Press this mixture through a sieve, discard skins. Return rest to cooking pot and add sugar, orange juice and gelatin. Stir over low until dissolved. Stir in liqueur. Turn into a 4 cup bowl. Chill in freezer (covered) about 1 1/2 hours. Then beat until creamy. Freeze about 2-3 hours. When serving, soften a wee bit first.

Cranberry Jelly

4 cups   cranberries
2 cups   sugar
1 cup   boiling water

Place cranberries in a saucepan and all the boiling water. Boil about 10 minutes until all the skins have burst. Mash through a sieve — collect pulp in pan and add sugar. Bring slowly to a boil, stirring constantly so that all the sugar is dissolved. Pour immediately into a wet mold or sterilized glasses.

Variation:
2 cups   cranberries
2 cups   boiling water
2 cups   sugar
dash   salt

Boil cranberries and water 15 minutes. Press through a sieve,then cook pulp another 3 minutes. Add sugar and salt and cook 2 more minutes. Pour into mould and chill.

**For Salad: when jelly begins to thicken, fold in
1 1/2 cups finely chopped celery.*

53.

Cranberry Sherbet

1 1/2 cups   cranberry jelly
1   lemon- grated rind only
1   lemon- juice
1   orange- juice
1/2 pint   cream, whipped

Using an ice cube tray (without racks), pack first mixture into tray(s). When the mixture is partially frozen but not solid, spoon it into a bowl. Whip the cream, and fold into first mixture until evenly blended. Spoon back into trays to finish freezing or can leave in bowl if it's metal.

Spicy Cranberry Relish

2 cups	cranberries
1/2 cup	white vinegar
2/3 cup	water
1 cup	brown sugar
1/2 tsp.	cloves
1/2 tsp.	ginger
1/2 tsp.	paprika
1 tsp.	cinnamon
1/2 tsp.	salt
dash	pepper
2 tbsps.	butter

Put first 3 ingredients in a cooking pot, and boil until the berries are soft (approx. 5 minutes). When cool, grind, or chop in blender. Add the sugar and spices. Simmer 3 more minutes, then add butter. Serve when cooled, but not chilled.

Cranberry Pickle

2/3 cup	cider vinegar
1/3 cup	water
2 cups	sugar
1/8 tsp.	salt
6 whole	cloves
1 stick	cinnamon
6	whole allspice
4 cups	cranberries

Tie spices in a piece of cheesecloth. Combine vinegar, sugar, water, salt and spice bag in a saucepan. Bring to a boil, then turn down to simmer for 10 minutes. Add berries, bring back to a boil, and then simmer till cooked. Pour into sterile jars and cover with paraffin wax.

Janet's Cranberry Liqueur

1 pound cranberries
1 1/2 cups sugar syrup *
1 1/2 cups vodka (375 ml)
1/4 of an orange — scrape and slice peel
half of a lemon — scrape and slice peel

Wash cranberries and coarsely chop in blender or food processor. Add all the ingredients to the alcohol. Steep 4 weeks. Strain and filter. If more sweetener is desired, add more sugar syrup to taste and mature another week.

*Sugar Syrup
1 cup white granulated sugar
1/2 cup water

Yields: 3-4 cups finished liqueur

INDEX

Starters

Muffins &Breads

Main Meals

Desserts

Additions

Celebrating Cranberries

Author Fern Walker is a native of Nova Scotia, who, as she says, grew up immersed in Wild Blueberry activities. Her father, Carvell Stonehouse, was involved in that industry for 51 years. Fern worked in the family business until moving to Kanata, Ontario with husband Paul and their children. She continued to do promotion for B.P.A.N.S. and W.B.A.N.A. In 1983, she started Fern's Frozen Fruit, a business geared for

Fund-Raising (for non-profit groups) dealing with I.Q.F. wild blueberries, raspberries and now — cranberries. People tend to think of cranberries mainly at Thanksgiving and Christmas but there are so many ways to enjoy this delicious fruit other than in sauces and drinks. Hence the idea for **CELEBRATING CRANBERRIES**, a cookbook with a variety of 60 recipes including Breakfast Cup, Cranberry Pecan Pie, Linzer Torte, Salads and exciting new Relishes.

CELEBRATING CRANBERRIES is Walker's second cookbook, her first being **BASICALLY BLUE**....a collection of blueberry recipes, a Canadian best-seller since 1993.

ISBN 0-9684596-0-9

9 780968 459607